Neo-Futuristic elongated pumpkin shaped building with arc shaped windows/doors.

NET CONES

Neo-Futuristic glass towers with white metal
skeletal walls.

MARSHMELLO

Contemporary artistic style home with white marshmallow facade.

RED SOLITUDE

Modern red home on a hill with a red spherical
dome for movies or etc.

DARK ELEGANCE

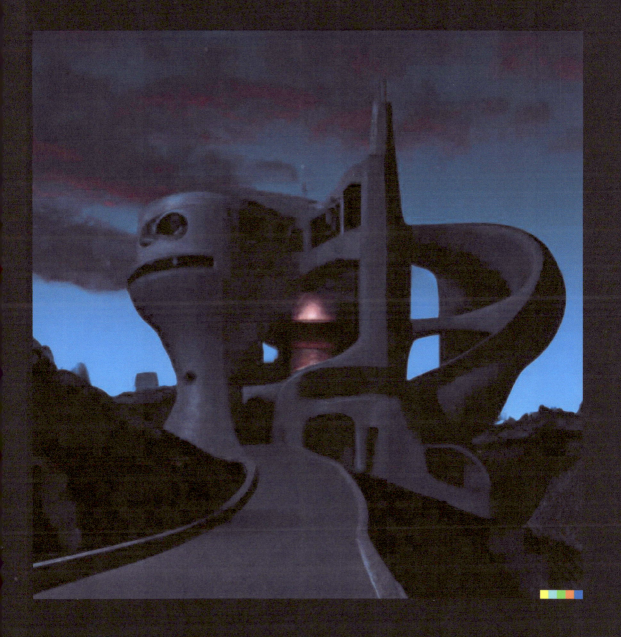

Neo-Futuristic mansion with elegant tunnels and oval design.

TESLA TOWER

Modern mansion in the Grand Canyon with a
Tesla coil.

HEXA-ORB

Art Deco dome home made of a hexagon metal
skeleton and smart glass.

PUMPKIN HOME

Postmodern pumpkin house with wooden craftsman details in a dark forest.

UFO MANSION

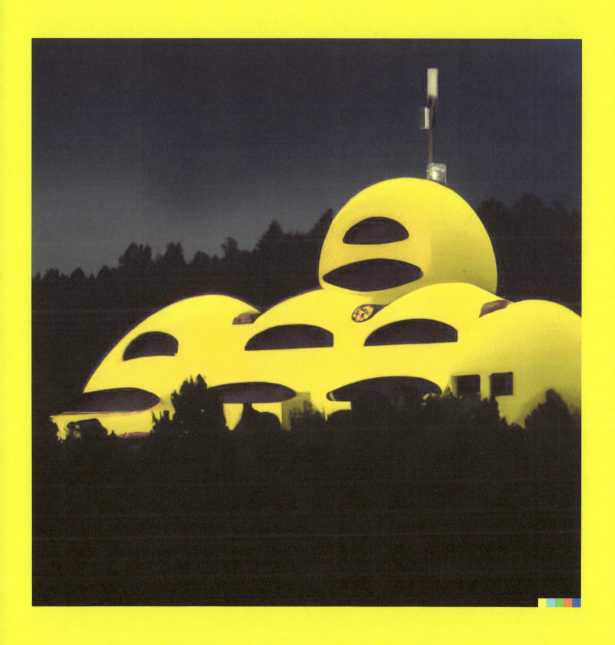

Neo-Futuristic yellow circular homes stuck
together with black windows.

BALANCE BE

Luxurious modern home with red details on a
pillar rock.

LUCIDEN

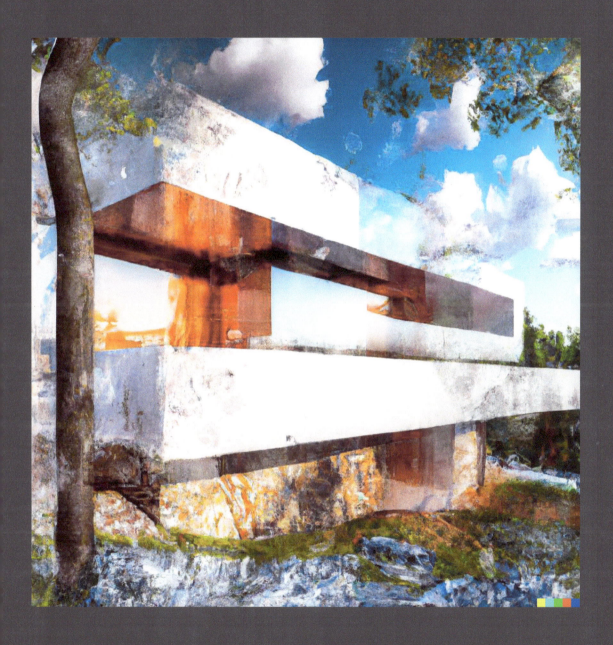

Simple modern home on a forest hill in white with orange windows.

CIRCU-LUXE

Contemporary luxe home in a rocky forest hill.

TRIGONO-HEDRON

Neo-Futuristic geodesic polyhedron home with textured facade.

TEAL TOWER

Postmodern teal tower with circle windows.

TRANSPERENCIA

Modern transparent building with smart glass
window walls.

UFO EGG

Neo-Futuristic egg shaped building with indented window and terrace holes.

TRYPOPHOBIC

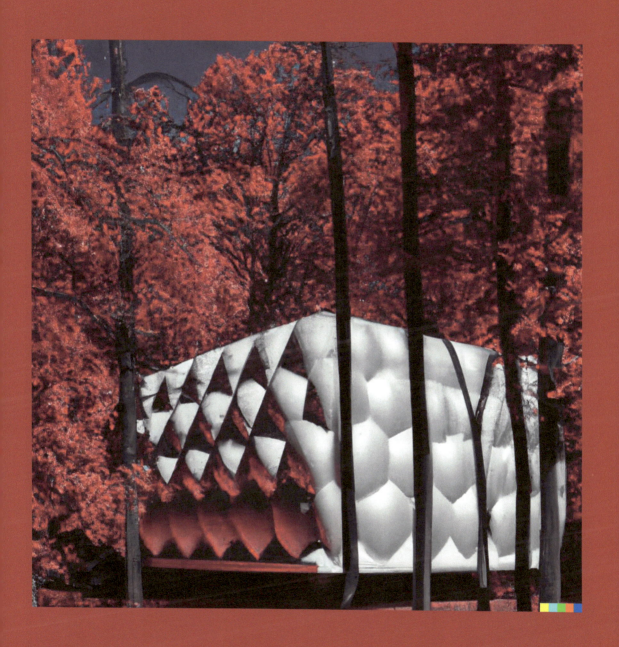

Neo-Futuristic building with glass bubble walls and windows.

LAPIS SPHERE

Art Deco sphere made of metal skeleton and blue
glass on a pillar.

INCAS

Brutalist cement home with geometric style and red windows.

DARKEST BANK

Brutalist art building with high door and a curtain
coming down and up.

PRIMARY PORTALS

Contemporary art style home in primary colors
and tinted windows.

SHIP-SCRAPER

Neo-Futuristic tall ship building with yellow lights and laser.

CAPSOULS

Postmodern cylinder homes with windmills.

WINE VILLA

Papilio Polyxenes

Postmodern jello inspired home with oval
windows and a pond.

CANDY CORNS

Neo-futuristic home made of glass in the shape of candy corn.

VIOLET VILLA

Contemporary art home tower on pillars with
circle windows.

OCEAN NEST

Art Deco mansion on pillars with artistic shape terraces and windows.

ULTRA PINK

Modern simple pink home with pink mirror
windows in the desert.

CORN MANSION

Modern oval home with glazed orange roof and
white facade.

TIP OF GOLD

Brutalist column home with golden detail and triangular windows.

INFINITY TOROUS

Contemporary art home with circular lit frames
folding the sliding windows.

ONYX

Neo-Futuristic black glass building with tilted
double roof design.

LAZER TOWER

Neo-Futuristic tower made of black glass and laser top for universe exploration.

METAPHYSICALITY

Modern artistic home with square and triangle
windows and cement color facade.

CRYSTAL APPLE

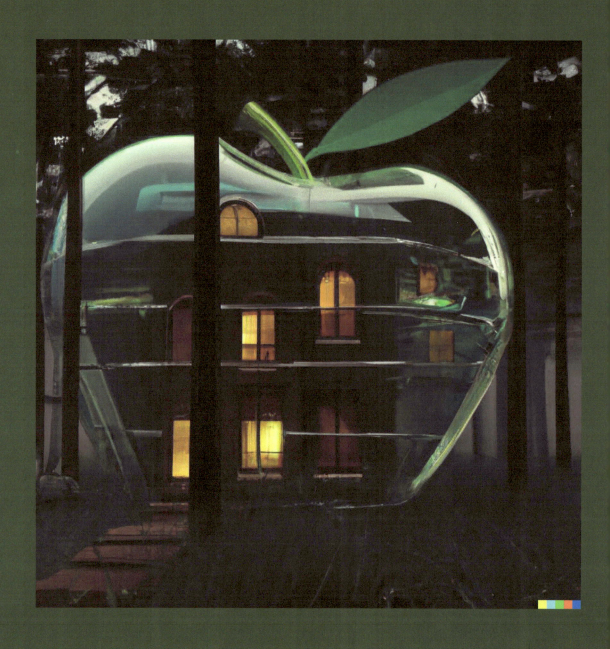

Neo-Futuristic house in shape of an apple made of glass panels.

RETRORANGE

Contemporary artistic home with oval windows
and door with underground space.

BAT LAB

Neo-Futuristic pyramid style building with tall
glass windows and metal bearings.

PUMPKIN CABIN

Postmodern pumpkin shaped home with circle
windows on sides and roof.

RETROGRADE

Modern circular building surrounding a grass
fiend and a path to both ends.

CRYMSON CABIN

American craftsman shed with two entrances in a grass field.

PINK TWILIGHT

Brutalist pink concrete building with big terraces and pillar.

ROBODOMES

Neo-Futuristic big domes with windows which
move with the sun 360 degrees.

MOON MANSION

Postmodern half moon shaped mansion on top of
a hill with long stairs.

CARNELIAN

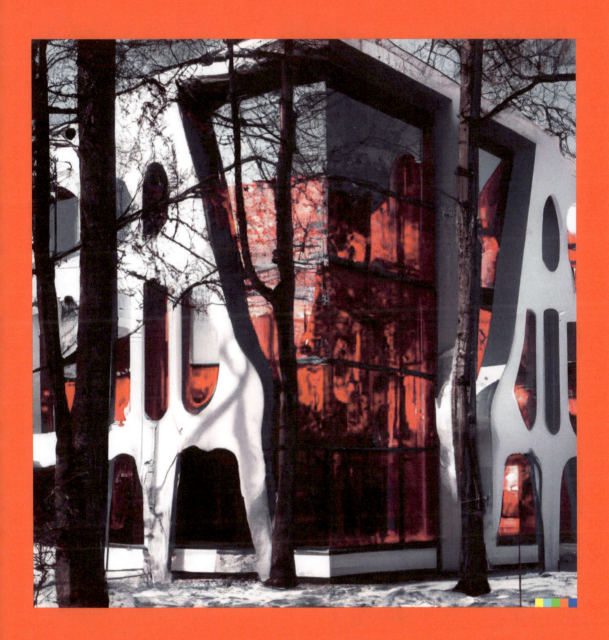

Neo-futuristic style mansion with red windows
and white intricate skeleton exterior.

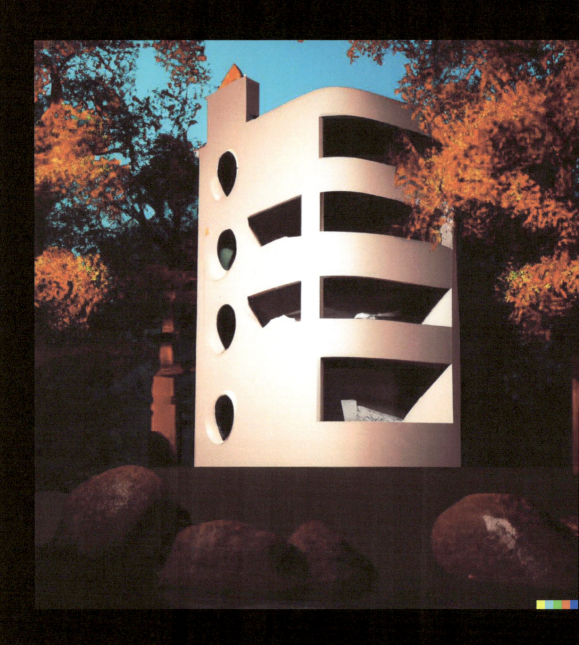

Art Deco home with circular windows and big terraces.

CYBER - LUXE

Neo-futuristic style mansion with gold cylinders and green traces on a mountain hill.

POP

Postmodern yellow intricate home with pink
columns and sharp roof.

CAKE QUEEN

Contemporary art house made to look like cake.

GOLDEN MOUNT

Modern gold colored building with X shape design view from space.

PUMPKIN GUILD

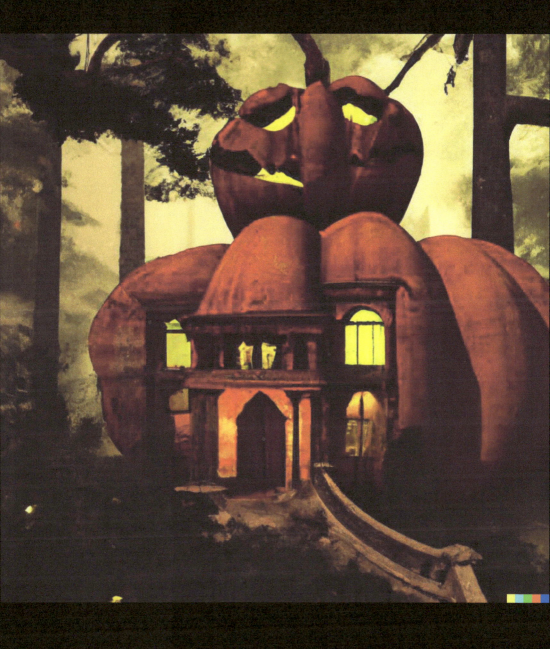

Postmodern pumpkin style mansion with a carved
windows head.

PHANTASM

Neo-Futuristic home shaped like space ship with pillars and long stairs.

MANGANITE

International style black and red building center
with spherical area with no windows.

PLUM VILLA

Luxurious modern home in purple and yellow windows.

OCTATOWER

Contemporary octagon shape tower home in teal
color and wood detail.

RUBIDIUM

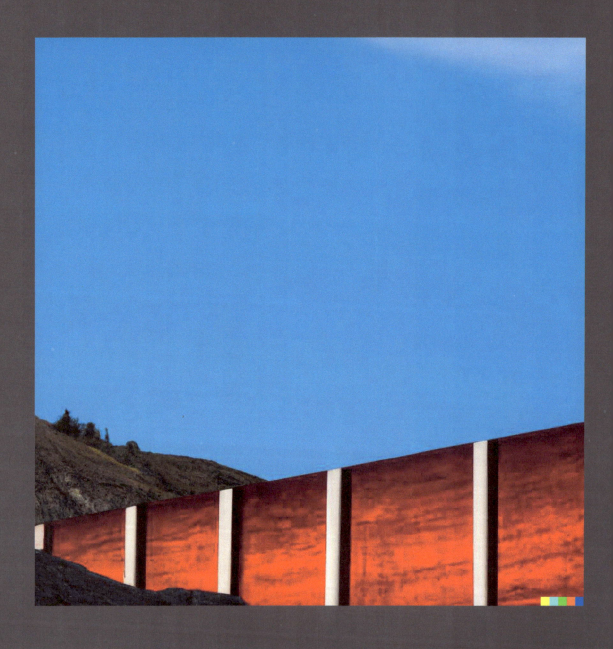

Art Deco luxe home made of only red windows up
to the roof.

VESPULA VULGARIS

Neo-Futuristic mega house with different shape
windows and terraces,

QUBOID

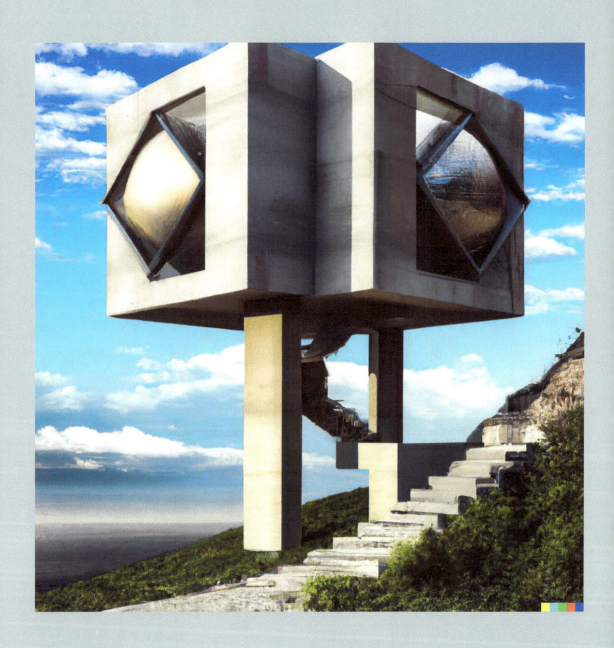

Brutalist square style home with oval windows
inside a square standing on pillars.

AQUATIC

Elegant contemporary style building with blue
glass windows on a hill.

CRYPTANTHUS

Art Deco retro home with black windows and pink facade.

OCULOS

Postmodern building with windows in shape of
eyes in a valley.

CORUNDUM

Contemporary home or library with deep red windows.

PENTADOME

Art Deco sphere made of pentagons with metal
skeleton and glass windows.

LANDING

Brutalist concrete building with big terraces
overlooking the desert.

INMOUNT

Modern house inside the hill.

HEARTSTONE

Neo-Futuristic house which looks like a heart from space.

TRILATERAL

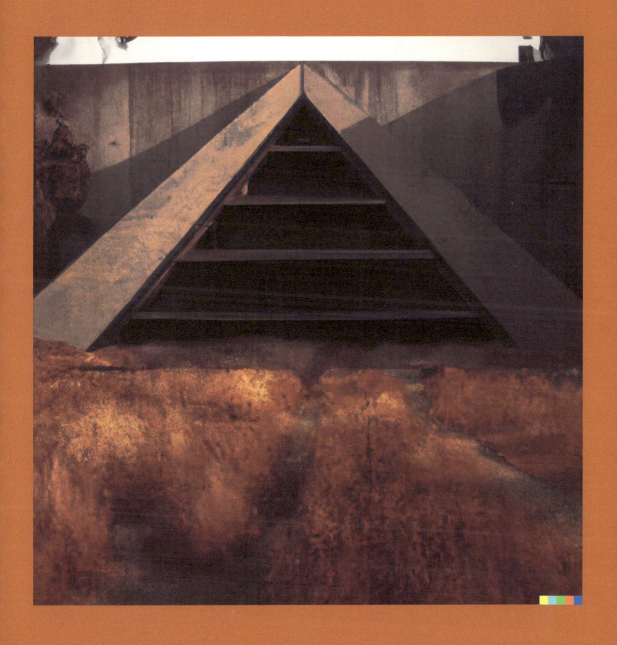

Brutalist building with triangular window and
garage door.

ORAPAD

Contemporary orange luxe building with artistic
windows.

GOURD

Modern marshmallow inspired home with oval
walls and windows.

PHANTOMA

Luxe Art Deco circular home with glass walls and statement art sphere in front.

SPHERE-NET

Art Deco sphere home with metal skeleton and circular windows.

CHIROPTERA

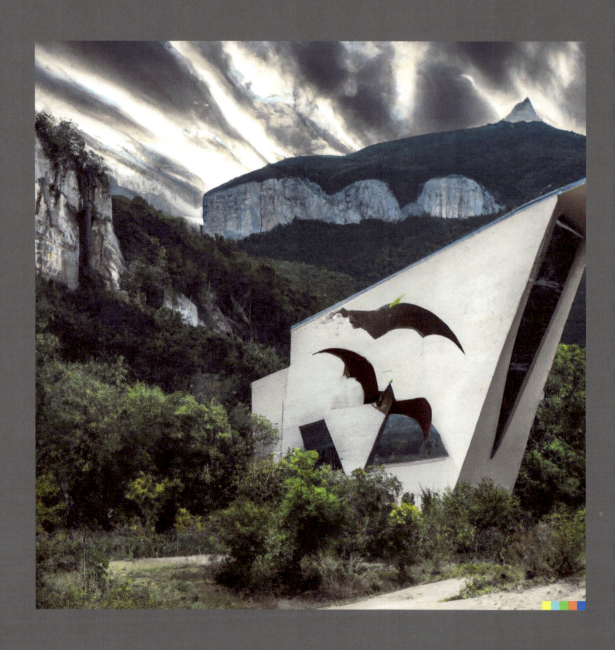

Brutalist luxurious building with artistic design
windows in the forest.

VITIS TOWER

American craftsman octagon tower made of brick with a side of vines.

LAPIS

Postmodern hill mansion with blue glass and
artistic shapes.

BLUE BEANS

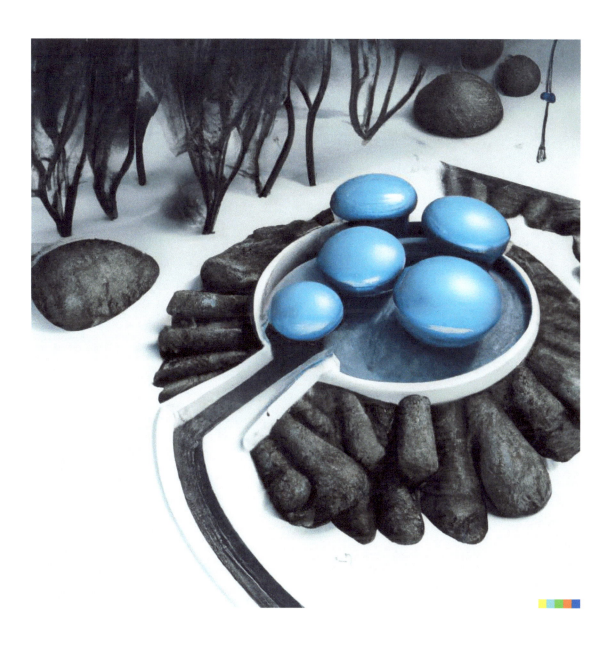

Brutalist artistic underground building with shiny
blue bean art entrance.

BUBBLE HOUSE

Modern home with bubbles shaped windows.

CUCURBITA

Contemporary art building inspired by a pumpkin
supported by 360 surrounded arcs.

PEAK

Brutalist mansion held by concrete columns on a hill, hidden in the natural environment.

DENSITY

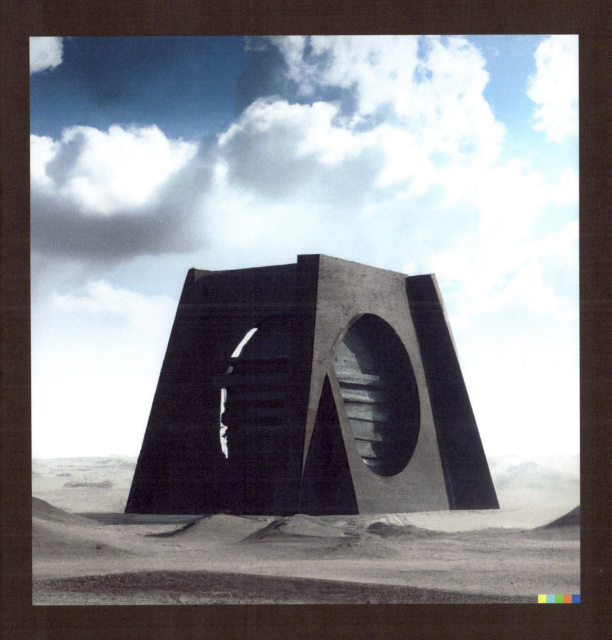

Brutalist building with special metal closing
windows in case of a sand storm.

PHOTON

Neo-Futuristic luxe home in shape of space craft
and nice terrace roof.

EARTHED

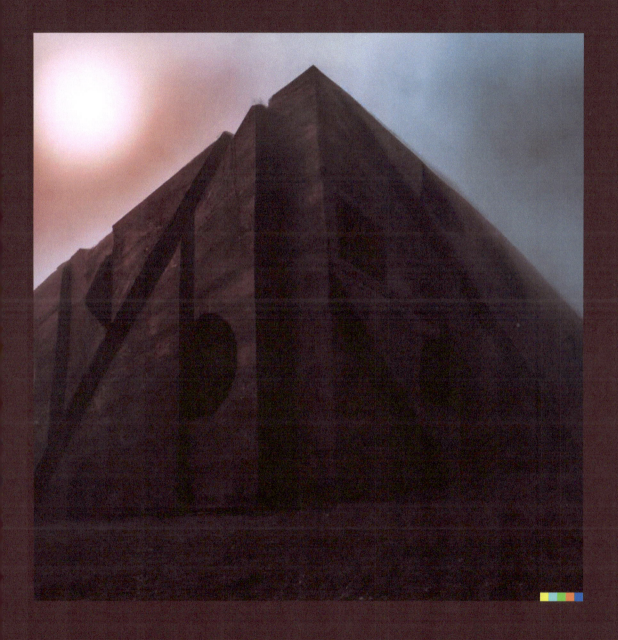

Brutalist solid brown cement building with
artistic facade and windows.

PERIDOT

Brutalist cement building with rock facade and
green smart glass windows.

BLUE DISK

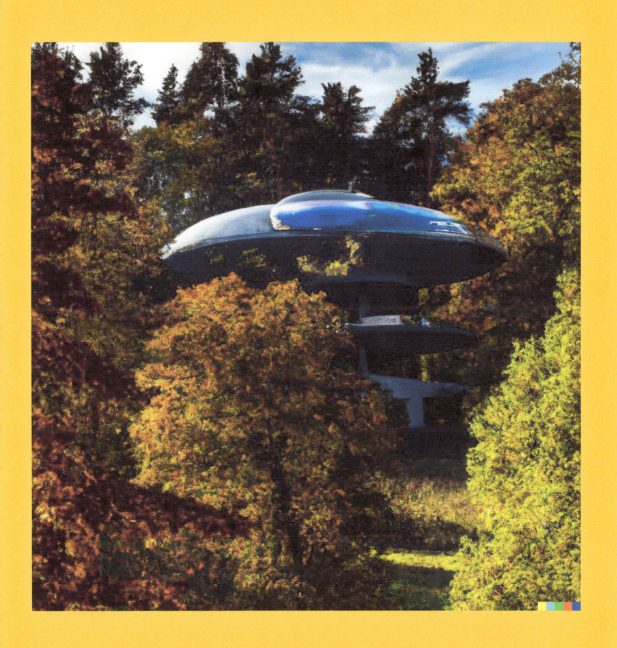

Neo-Futuristic ufo shaped home with big glass
roof in an autumn forest.

FLOAT

Neo-Futuristic home which lifts up and down
thanks to the elevation system.

CORDIAL

Brutalist style building in the forest with black facade and orange windows.

BORON

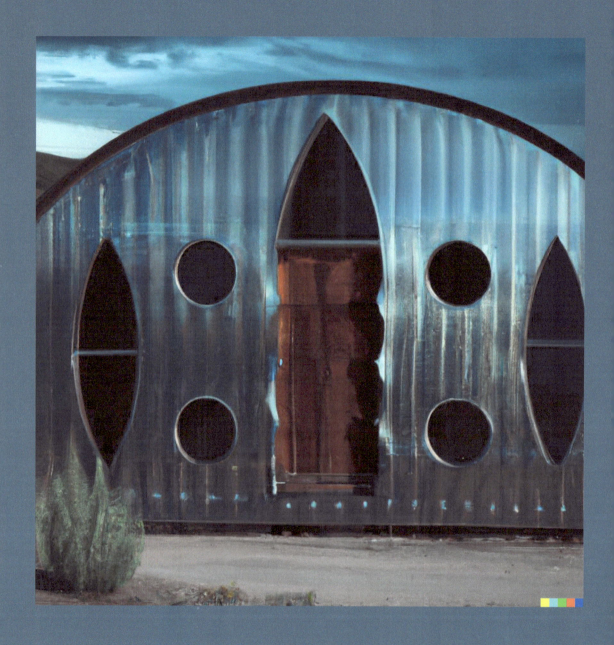

Art Deco cylinder home with artistic windows in the desert.

LANTERN

Contemporary mansion inspired by a pumpkin
with big circular windows.

DISCOID

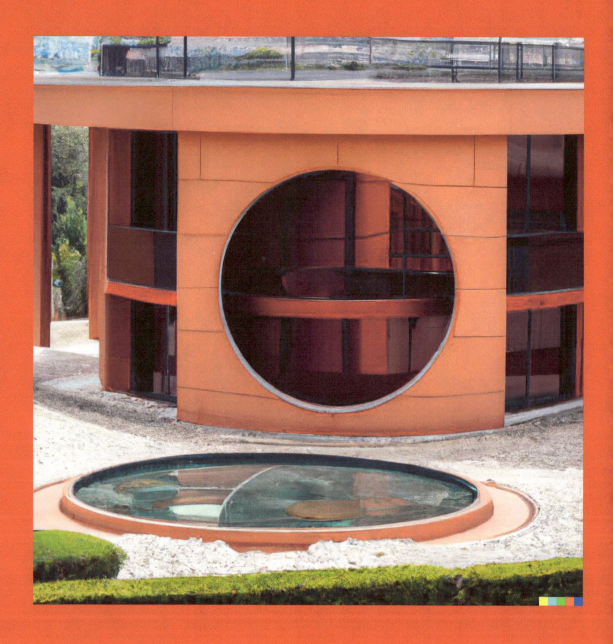

Red modern circular home with roof terrace and circle art pool.

CRYMSON HILL

Classical luxe mansion with columns in a red field.

OVOID

Modern Art Deco home with sphere window in a
birch forest.

PAPUSTYLA

Contemporary green home with snail eyes and
luxe design.

CANDY CORN

Luxe Art Deco home in candy corn shape in an
autumn forest.

GARNET

Art Deco home made of steel and red glass in a dark forest.

HIDEN

Brutalist concrete tower made to protect and hide people.

DARKEN

Second empire dark modern black skeleton
building.

PYRAMOUNT

Brutalist concrete piramid lab in the forest.

WHALE MANSION

ICOSAHEDOME

Art Deco dome sphere made of glass triangles and steel bearings.

LANDING TOWER

Brutalist square tower with sphere window
overlooking from a mountain top.

MAGIC APPLE

Postmodern cone tower and contemporary apple
home in a forest.

WEEN

Contemporary black wooden home with
underground area.

OBSEDIAN

Spooky Art Deco house wit red glass in the forest.

GLASS POP

luxe tower home with glass surface.

FIBONACCI

Sustainable art building looking like romansco broccoli.

CANDY CORN

Modern residency with a yellow cob entrance in
an autumn forest.

INFINITY TOROUS

Art Deco mansion under a circular roof with a big fire pit.

GREEN HOUSE

Sustainable modern house with moss facade and electric panels.

PURPURE

Contemporary house in purple in a deep dark forest.

SHIP LAB

Brutalist lab looking like a space ship on a hill.

BLACK EYES

Postmodern yellow home in oval shape with black
circular windows in the desert.

THE BLACK

Modern futuristic home in black and wooden doors.

TIP TOWER

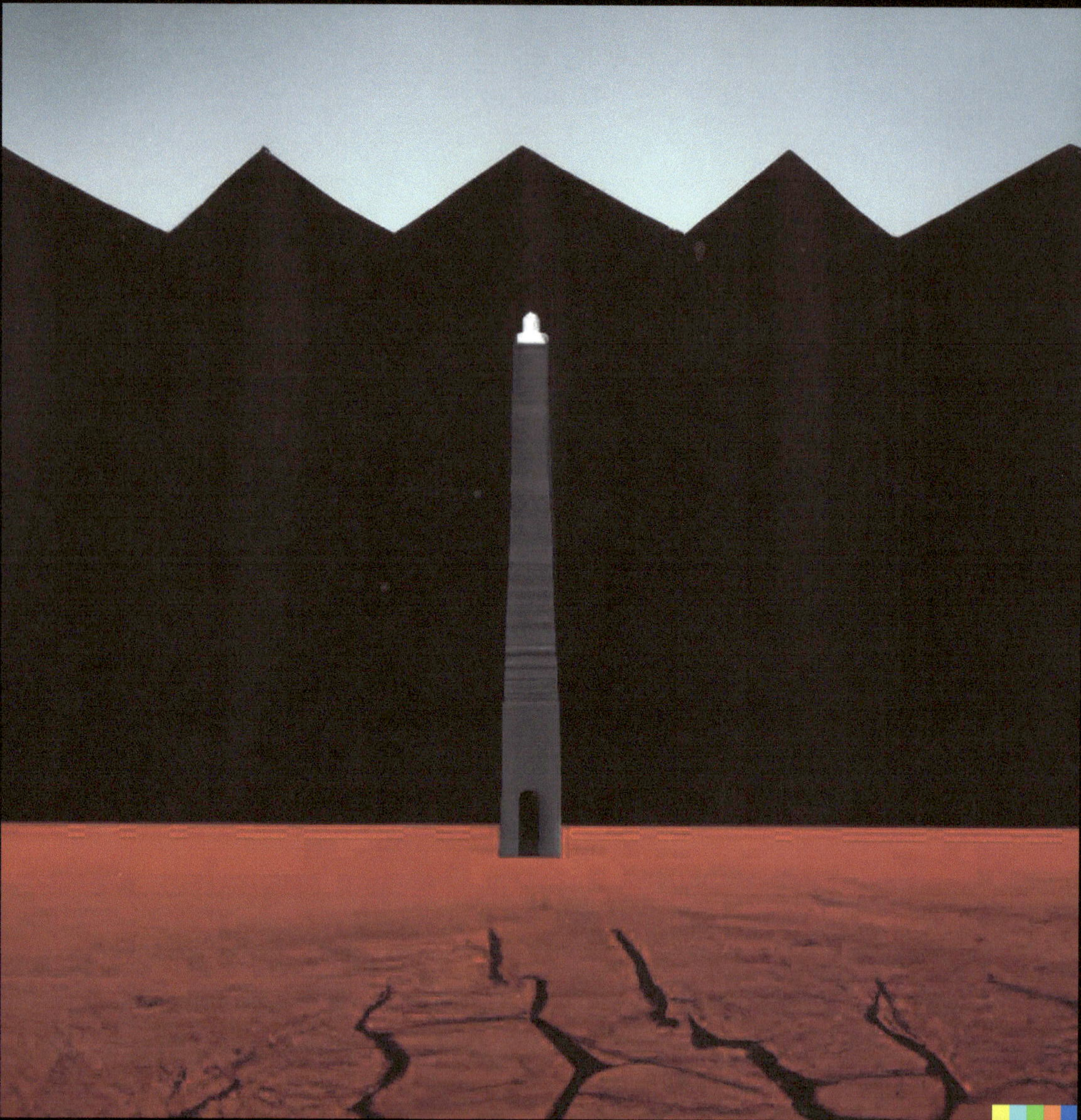

DEEP DARK

Modern ultra black mansion in an orange desert
with white sphere statues.

CUBIK

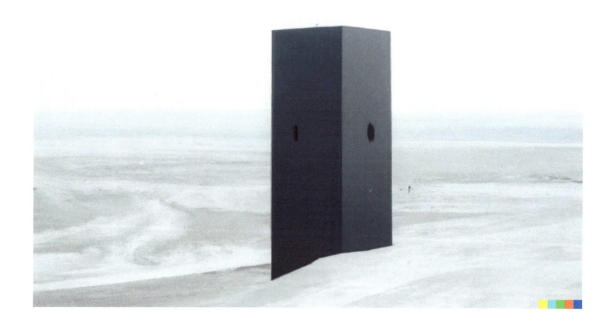

Contemporary black steel cuboid building in a white desert.

BONE SPHERE

Postmodern golf ball made of small skeletal
structure on an ocean hill.

WATER PYRAMID

Brutalist pyramid with windows peaking out of
the water.

ALTITUDE

Cyber-punk one pillar home in an autumn forest.

BLIMP BUILDING

Contemporary red blimp inspired mansion in the middle of a forest.

www.ingramcontent.com/pod-product-compliance
Lightning Source LLC
LaVergne TN
LVHW060201050326
832903LV00016B/332